P9-CQN-057

Courageous Heroes
of the American West

Buffalo Bill Cody
Courageous Wild West Showman

William R. Sanford and Carl R. Green

Enslow Publishers, Inc.
40 Industrial Road
Box 398
Berkeley Heights, NJ 07922
USA

http://www.enslow.com

Original edition published as *Buffalo Bill Cody: Showman of the Wild West* in 1996.

Library of Congress Cataloging-in-Publication Data

Sanford, William R. (William Reynolds), 1927–

   Buffalo Bill Cody : courageous wild west showman / William R. Sanford and Carl R. Green.

      p. cm. — (Courageous heroes of the American West)

   Original edition has subtitle: Showman of the Wild West.

   Includes index.

   Summary: "Explores Buffalo Bill Cody, including his childhood; working as a scout, buffalo hunter, and Pony Express rider; the creation and performances of his Wild West Show and his legacy in American history"—Provided by publisher.

   ISBN 978-0-7660-4007-6

   1. Buffalo Bill, 1846–1917—Juvenile literature. 2. Pioneers—West (U.S.)—Biography—Juvenile literature. 3. Entertainers—United States—Biography—Juvenile literature. 4. West (U.S.)—Biography—Juvenile literature. 5. Buffalo Bill's Wild West Show—History—Juvenile literature. I. Green, Carl R. II. Title.

   F594.B63S36 2012

   978'.02092—dc23

   [B]

2011031052

Future editions:

Paperback ISBN 978-1-4644-0090-2

ePUB ISBN 978-1-4645-0997-1

PDF ISBN 978-1-4646-0997-8

Printed in the United States of America

032012 Lake Book Manufacturing, Inc., Melrose Park, IL

10 9 8 7 6 5 4 3 2 1

To Our Readers: We have done our best to make sure all Internet addresses in this book were active and appropriate when we went to press. However, the author and the publisher have no control over, and assume no liability for, the material available on those Internet sites or on other Web sites they may link to. Any comments or suggestions can be sent by e-mail to comments@enslow.com or to the address on the back cover.

Enslow Publishers, Inc., is committed to printing our books on recycled paper. The paper in every book contains 10% to 30% post-consumer waste (PCW). The cover board on the outside of each book contains 100% PCW. Our goal is to do our part to help young people and the environment too!

Illustration Credits: Buffalo Bill Historical Center, Cody, Wyoming, U.S.A.; Garlow Collection, P.69.2078, p. 7; Enslow Publishers, Inc., p. 11; © Enslow Publishers, Inc. / Paul Daly, p. 1; Everett Collection, pp. 15, 21; Library of Congress Prints and Photographs, pp. 19, 26, 30, 34, 36, 39, 43.

Cover Illustration: © Enslow Publishers, Inc. / Paul Daly.

Contents

Authors' Note

This book tells the true story of William F. Cody. Most people know him by his famous nickname, Buffalo Bill. He was one of the Wild West's greatest heroes. He was a brave and resourceful scout, a buffalo hunter, and a distinguished showman. During his lifetime, he was the subject of hundreds of dime novels. In more recent years, he has been brought to life in dozens of films and television productions. You may doubt that one man could pack so much adventure into a single lifetime. If so, rest easy. All of the events described in this book actually happened.

Chapter 1

Riding for the Pony Express

Fourteen-year-old Bill Cody crouched low as his horse galloped across Wyoming Territory. Like all Pony Express riders, he was paid to cover fifteen miles an hour. Horse Creek Station lay a mile behind the young mail carrier. A fresh horse waited for him at Sweetwater Bridge.

Bill's horse thundered through a ravine. Without warning, a band of American Indian warriors swarmed down the sides of the ravine. Rifles barked. Bullets whistled past Bill's head. The boy flattened himself on the horse's back. Reaching for more speed, he put spurs and whip to his mount. Luckily, he was riding one of the station's fastest horses.

With his pursuers two miles behind, Bill pulled up at Sweetwater Bridge. Instead of a fresh horse, he found a dead station keeper. The corral was empty.

Bill pushed his tired horse on to Plant's Station. A change of mounts was waiting for him. "I finished the trip without any further adventure," he wrote later.

Bill rode for the firm of Russell, Majors, and Waddell. He was one of eighty riders who carried the mail from St. Joseph, Missouri, to Sacramento, California. The old mail route had curved southward through Texas and Arizona. Letters sent by that route took twenty-five days to reach San Francisco. The Pony Express cut delivery time to ten days. The riders galloped across prairie, desert, and mountains.

Wagon master George Chrisman gave Bill his first job with the Pony Express. The boy assured his boss that he had been raised in the saddle. As a test, Chrisman assigned Bill to a short forty-five-mile leg out of Julesburg, Colorado. Bill proved his worth by finishing the rugged ride on time. His light weight, he said, was easy on the horses. Some months later, stage agent Alf Slade took a liking to the boy. Slade put Bill on the seventy-six-mile leg from Red Buttes to Three Crossings, Wyoming.

Like all the riders, Bill carried mail in pouches sewn into a sheet of leather. This *mochila* was cut to fit over the saddle's wooden frame. As Bill sped into a station, he pulled the mochila out from under him.

Buffalo Bill was only fourteen years old when he became a Pony Express rider. To keep his schedule, he would sometimes ride seventy-five miles or more a day. Bill was nineteen when he posed for this photo.

After a quick dismount, he threw it onto a waiting horse. A station agent scribbled on his time card. A moment later, Bill was off again.

Bone-jarring rides of seventy-six miles were all in a day's work. Bill earned Slade's praise with a greater show of endurance. On reaching Three Crossings one day, he found that the relief rider had been killed in a brawl. Bill jumped on a fresh horse and set out for Rocky Ridge, eighty-five miles away. There he picked up the eastbound mochila and retraced his route. The round trip totaled 322 miles. "My boy," Slade told him, "you're a brick, and no mistake. That was a good run you made." Coming from a tough boss like Slade, that was high praise.

In June 1861, Bill left the Pony Express to be with his ailing mother. On October 24, workers finished the first cross-country telegraph line. Sending a message from New York to San Francisco now took only minutes. The Pony Express could not compete. The bankrupt line shut down in November.

Years later, Buffalo Bill brought the Pony Express back to life in his Wild West show. Daring riders helped cheering crowds relive the drama of the horseback mail service. Buffalo Bill knew the Pony Express as well as anyone alive. As the teenage Bill Cody, he had *been* a Pony Express rider.

Chapter 2

A Boy Grows Up Fast on the Frontier

Just like many young people of their day, Isaac Cody and Mary Ann Laycock wanted elbow room. In 1840, the newlyweds moved to the Iowa Territory. The young couple built a four-room log cabin near Le Claire. Samuel was born in 1841, Julia in 1843. On February 26, 1846, Mary gave birth to William Frederick Cody. Her pet name for the baby was Billy. His brother and sisters called him Willy. As a teenager, the boy set the matter straight. He told people to call him Bill.

Danger was a fact of life on a frontier farm. In 1853, a skittish mare reared up, threw Samuel, and fell back on him. The boy died the next day. To take his wife's mind off her grief, Bill's father moved the family to Kansas.

At Fort Leavenworth, Kansas, Bill saw his first American Indians. He felt an even greater thrill when he saw soldiers drilling their well-trained horses. Before long, his father gave him a half-wild Indian pony named Prince. Horace Billings, Bill's uncle, helped the boy tame his new mount. Horace also taught Bill how to throw a lasso.

For a while, all went well. The Codys built a seven-room log cabin at Salt Creek Valley. Isaac won a contract to supply hay to Fort Leavenworth.

In May 1854, Congress passed a law that touched off years of strife. The law gave Kansas the right to choose to be a free state or a slave state. That set off a race to settle the territory. Proslavers and antislavers hurried to stake their claims.

That September, Bill and his father passed a proslavery rally. The leaders stopped Isaac and forced him to speak to the crowd. His father, Bill wrote later, said he opposed the spread of slavery. That was too much for one proslave hothead. The man stabbed Isaac in the chest. Eight-year-old Bill helped carry his father to the nearby trading post.

Isaac survived, but bands of proslavers were hunting for him. He went into hiding. Unable to find their man, the raiders stole the Codys' livestock and burned their hay. But their anger did not stop there. Bill and his sisters had been going to a country school.

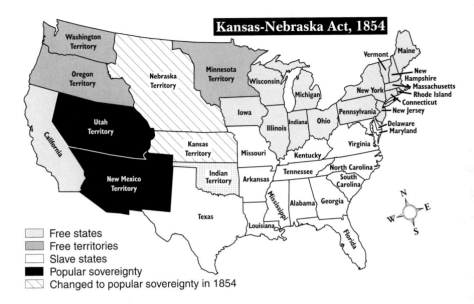

Kansas-Nebraska Act, 1854

Washington Territory
Oregon Territory
Nebraska Territory
Minnesota Territory
Wisconsin
Vermont
Maine
New Hampshire
Massachusetts
Rhode Island
Connecticut
New Jersey
Michigan
New York
Pennsylvania
Utah Territory
Iowa
Indiana
Ohio
Delaware
Maryland
Illinois
California
Kansas Territory
Missouri
Kentucky
Virginia
New Mexico Territory
Indian Territory
Arkansas
Tennessee
North Carolina
South Carolina
Texas
Mississippi
Alabama
Georgia
Louisiana
Florida

Free states
Free territories
Slave states
Popular sovereignty
Changed to popular sovereignty in 1854

The passage of the Kansas-Nebraska Act had a dramatic impact on Bill's family. The proslavers who flooded into Kansas often attacked anyone who held abolitionist beliefs—a group that included Bill's father, Isaac. This map shows the affect of the Kansas-Nebraska Act on the United States.

The teacher fled when angry proslavers threatened to burn the school to the ground.

To help feed the family, Bill planted ten acres of corn. When he was not tending the crop, he hunted rabbits and squirrels. He needed his hunting rifle the night a killer came looking for his father. Isaac, Bill knew, was upstairs, too sick to leave his bed. The boy stood guard at the head of the stairs, ready to shoot. Bill's mother calmed the man by feeding him a good supper. He left at last, still vowing to kill "her damned abolitionist husband."

Isaac died of pneumonia in the spring of 1857. The Codys blamed his death on the old stab wound. With Isaac gone, the family was short of cash. Mary sold the horses and put the farm up for rent. A neighbor hired Bill to haul supplies to Leavenworth for fifty cents a day. When that job ended, Bill found work carrying messages. The pay was good, but he hated the sitting and waiting. John Willis, a friendly wagon boss, gave him a better job. Bill tended Willis's oxen each time the teams returned from a trip.

That winter, Mary sent Bill back to school. The fee was two dollars a month. In the spring, he fell in love with Mary Hyatt. To please her, he built a playhouse in the schoolyard. An older boy named Steve Gobel kicked it down. In the fight that followed, Steve pinned Bill against a wall. Bill pulled out a pocketknife and slashed the bully's thigh. Steve ran to the teacher, screaming that he had been killed. That night, a constable came looking for Bill.

Bill hid out while John Willis talked to Mary Cody about her son's problem. She agreed that Bill should join Willis on a trip to Fort Kearny. "The trip was a most enjoyable one for me," Bill reported. "No incidents of note occurred on the way." The fight was forgotten by the time the wagon train returned home.

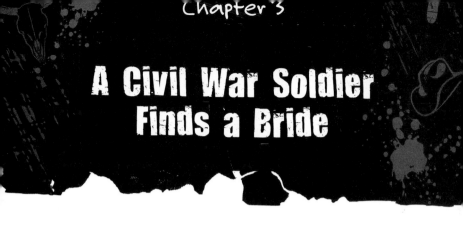

Chapter 3

A Civil War Soldier Finds a Bride

The conflict over slavery soon engulfed the nation. The first shots of the Civil War rang out in April 1861. Bill Cody, fresh from his work for the Pony Express, could have served as a drummer boy. Many fifteen-year-olds wore Northern blue or Southern gray. It was his mother, ill with consumption, who stood in his way. She made him promise not to join up while she lived.

The promise kept Bill out of uniform, but not out of trouble. Kansas had become a free state, but slavery still existed across the border in Missouri. When a band of Kansans planned a raid on Missouri farms, Bill rode with them. Perhaps he hoped to avenge his father's death. The raiders, he soon learned, were mostly out to steal horses.

As Bill wrote later: "We didn't let our consciences trouble us very much." Mary Cody learned that several raiders had been sent to jail. She ordered Bill to quit the band. He obeyed.

Heading west again, Bill met two of the Wild West's greatest heroes. The first was a scout named Wild Bill Hickok. Hickok hired the boy to help haul freight. In St. Louis, the two lost all their money betting on a horse race. In the spring of 1862, Bill served as guide and scout with the Ninth Kansas Volunteers. The troop's task was to keep the Santa Fe Trail open. In New Mexico, he was awed by the famous mountain man Kit Carson. Years later, Bill named his son Kit Carson Cody.

In 1863, Bill left the volunteers to join a wagon train bound for Denver. Word reached him there that his mother was gravely ill. He returned home in time to say goodbye before she died.

The Seventh Kansas Volunteers came home on leave in February 1864. His friends in the troop urged Bill to enlist. He turned them down but joined them for a drinking spree. "One morning I awoke to find myself a soldier," he wrote. "I did not remember how or when I had enlisted, but I saw I was in for it."

Army records say that Private Cody served in Company H. His hair and eyes are listed as brown, his height as five feet ten inches. In June, the regiment

The famous frontiersman Wild Bill Hickok once hired young Bill Cody to help him haul freight. The two men became good friends, but lost all their money betting on a horse race in St. Louis.

marched south to guard a key rail line. On July 14, Bill took part in a major battle. The Union army turned back the Confederates that day at Tupelo, Mississippi.

In September, the regiment moved north. Private Cody was detailed to serve as a scout. On one trip behind rebel lines, he described a meeting with a gray-clad stranger. To his surprise, the "Southerner" turned out to be Wild Bill Hickok. His old friend gave him a packet of reports to take back. Did those reports help the North turn back a Southern advancement toward St. Louis? Bill thought they did.

That winter, the army assigned Bill to a St. Louis hospital. In his off-duty hours, he met Louisa Federici. Bill wrote: "I adored her above any young lady I had ever seen." As a joke on one of her boyfriends, the two pretended to be engaged.

Bill left the service in September, still a private. Short of cash, he took a job driving horses to Fort Kearny, Nebraska. Next, he worked as a stagecoach driver. It was Louisa's letters that drew him east again. The joke engagement had turned serious. She was urging him to give up his wild life. Keep your promise to marry me, she told him.

Bill was dressed in western buckskins when he reached St. Louis. He was growing a mustache and a goatee. On March 6, 1866, he married Louisa. That same day, the newlyweds boarded a steamboat for Leavenworth. They were in love, but they were not well matched. Louisa wanted a quiet life. Only twenty years old, Bill yearned for open spaces and adventure.

In an attempt to please Louisa, Bill opened a hotel. The venture lasted only six money-losing months. Bill sold out and headed back to the plains. A tearful Louisa returned to St. Louis.

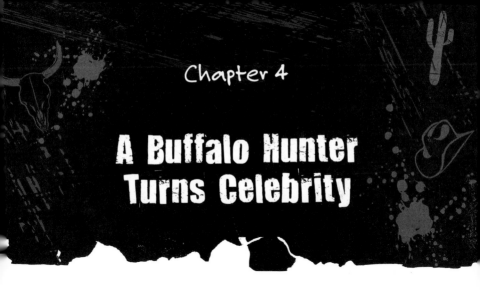

Chapter 4

A Buffalo Hunter Turns Celebrity

The turning point in Bill's life came in 1867. After Louisa gave up urging him to settle down, he went to work for the railroad. One day, he was grading a rail bed. His horse, Brigham, was pulling the heavy grader. When Bill spotted a herd of buffalo, he unhitched the horse. Rifle in hand, he set out to shoot some buffalo for the work crew's supper.

As he neared the herd, Bill met some army officers. They laughed and told him that his workhorse would never catch the herd. One of the men even offered to shoot a buffalo for him.

That was when Bill dropped Brigham's reins, leaving both hands free. Moments later, he was closing on the herd. The soldiers fell back, unable to match Brigham's speed. Bill dropped the closest buffalo with a single rifle shot. One by one, he killed ten more. The hunt ended; he gave the officers a share of the meat.

That fall, the railroad hired Bill to shoot twelve buffalo a day. The meat was used to feed the work crews. Bill enjoyed the challenge. At $1.67 a head, he earned $500 a month. Later, he wrote: "During my engagement as hunter for the company—a period of less than eighteen months—I killed 4,280 buffaloes." The well-fed work crews soon made up a song to sing when he passed by:

Buffalo Bill, Buffalo Bill
Never missed and never will.
Always aims and shoots to kill
And the company pays his buffalo bill.

Cody said it was these workmen who first called him Buffalo Bill. Others suggested it was the army officers at Fort Hayes. A third story credits dime-novel author Ned Buntline. As the story goes, Buntline needed a new hero for his novels. At Fort Sedgwick, he heard about Bill Cody's exploits. When Buntline found him, Cody was asleep under a wagon. Their meeting led to an 1869 tale called *Buffalo Bill, King of Border Men*. The novel was only the first of many. Over the years, Bill's adventures inspired more than five hundred dime novels.

Bill claimed to have killed 4,280 buffaloes in less than eighteen months. It was around this time that Bill was given his nickname. It is still unclear who officially gave him the name "Buffalo Bill," but it stuck. From that day on, Bill used it proudly and profitably.

Cody claimed that he won $300 and the title of Champion Buffalo Hunter in a shootoff. Officers at Fort Wallace backed their scout, Billy Comstock. The men at Fort Hayes put their money on Bill. During the eight-hour match, the hunters closed in on four small herds. Thanks to Brigham, Bill was able to drive his buffalo in a tight circle. Comstock chased his buffalo straight across the plain. Bill got off more shots—and he seldom missed. The final score read Buffalo Bill 69, Comstock 46.

In May 1868, Bill signed on as an army scout. The job soon tested him to the utmost. In a sixty-hour ride, he carried dispatches across three hundred and fifty miles of American Indian territory. General Philip Sheridan was impressed. He named Bill as chief scout for the Fifth Cavalry. The pay was equal to that paid an army colonel. Bill said that if he was drawing the pay, he deserved the title. In later life, he often called himself Colonel Cody.

Bill lived the rugged life of a scout for the next four years. In 1872, he was called on to help fight the Sioux. While scouting with six soldiers, Bill found the camp of a Sioux war party. Both sides opened fire. Pinpoint shooting killed three warriors. As the soldiers charged, the other warriors tried to flee. The pursuit

Author Ned Buntline helped build Buffalo Bill's fame when he featured him in his dime novels. Over the years, Bill starred in hundreds of these action-packed stories. This cover shows Buffalo Bill bravely fighting off a war party of American Indians.

almost ended when the soldiers' horses balked at jumping a creek. Bill's horse cleared it, and he took up the chase. Moments later, he shot two of the Sioux from their mounts. The others fled. For his bravery, Bill won the Congressional Medal of Honor.

History later added a strange footnote to that story. In 1916, Congress voted to strike Bill's name from the list of medal holders. What was the reason? The nation's highest honor, the lawmakers ruled, was meant only for members of the armed forces. Bill, hired as a scout, had been a civilian. Congress reversed itself and restored the medal in 1989—seventy-two years after Bill's death.

In 1872, Bill was very much alive. That fall, friends put him on the ballot for the Nebraska legislature. To his surprise, he won by forty-four votes. His career in politics did not last long. A recount gave the seat to his opponent. Bill was free to return to the life he loved best.

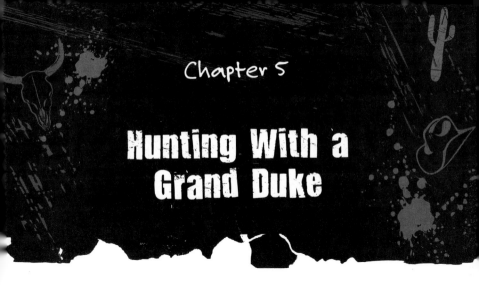

Chapter 5

Hunting With a Grand Duke

During his years as a scout, the army found other uses for Bill's talents. When the Fifth Cavalry was sent to Arizona to fight the Apache late in 1871, Bill did not join the troop. That summer, he had served as guide for a party of wealthy easterners. The hunt had been a smashing success. In November, General Sheridan sent Bill to take part in a once-in-a-lifetime event.

The Grand Duke Alexis, son of the Russian czar, was touring the United States. When Duke Alexis said he wanted to shoot buffalo, the government ordered a royal hunt. At Sheridan's command, Bill took charge. First, he picked out a campsite near Fort McPherson, Nebraska. Soldiers hurried to build Camp Alexis on a grassy knoll above Red Willow Creek. As Bill would say, it was a "dude's camp." The tents had wooden floors, carpets, and wood-burning stoves.

To add zest, Bill asked Spotted Tail, a Sioux chief, to join the hunt. The chief brought a large band of warriors with him. On the first night in camp, the Sioux staged a war dance. The grand duke and his party were delighted. Duke Alexis even flirted with a Sioux maiden.

January 14, 1872, was the grand duke's twenty-first birthday. He rode out mounted on Bill's best horse, Buckskin Joe. Shortly after nine o'clock, the party sighted a small herd of buffalo. Duke Alexis rode to within twenty feet and fired six wild pistol shots. None hit their mark. Bill handed the grand duke his pistol. Six more shots produced six more misses.

By custom, the royal guest had to make the first kill. Bill gave the grand duke his rifle and slapped Buckskin Joe on the rump. The well-trained horse sprinted forward. As he closed on a big bull, the grand duke aimed and fired. The bull dropped. Duke Alexis waved his hat as the rest of the party cheered.

A few news stories claimed that it was Bill Cody who killed the buffalo. Bill denied the reports, as did others who were there. What is certain is that the grand duke broke out the champagne to toast his kill.

Cody later wrote, "I was in hopes that he would kill five or six more buffaloes . . . if a basket of champagne was to be opened every time he dropped one."

Chinese lanterns hung from the trees above the camp that night. The camp chefs prepared a special meal. The first course was buffalo tail soup. Next came broiled fish, prairie dog sausage, and stewed rabbit. The grand duke ate a large tender slice of buffalo hump. The menu also included roast elk, deer, and wild turkey. Champagne, whiskey, brandy, and ale flowed freely.

The hunt lasted five days. In all, the grand duke bagged eight buffalo. A high point came the day the Sioux showed how they killed buffalo with bows and arrows. Duke Alexis rewarded Spotted Tail with a gift of one thousand barrels of tobacco. Each night, the hunters gathered around blazing campfires. Bill kept the Russians spellbound with his stories.

On the last day, Bill rode to the train with the grand duke and General Sheridan. Four half-trained cavalry horses pulled the open carriage. Hearing that Bill had once been a stage driver, the grand duke asked him to take the reins. "Shake 'em up a little," Sheridan ordered. Bill soon had the team flying over the rough ground. Their speed increased when they hit a long

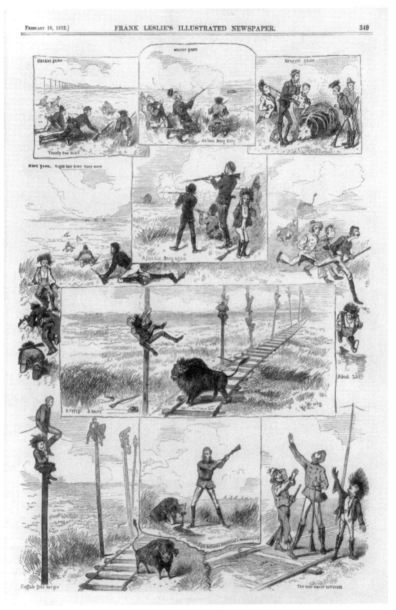

This cartoon published in *Frank Leslie's Illustrated Newspaper* on February 10, 1872, depicts the Grand Duke Alexis's buffalo hunt.

downhill slope. Without a brake, Bill could only keep the horses running straight ahead. He claimed later that he covered three miles in six minutes. A shaken grand duke said he preferred to "go a little slower."

On parting, Duke Alexis tried to give Bill a roll of greenbacks. Bill turned down the offer, but he did accept the grand duke's fine fur coat. Later, Alexis sent him a set of cuff links and a scarf pin. The pin, made in the shape of a buffalo head, was set with diamonds.

The world's press reported each day of the hunt. Buffalo Bill was becoming a household name. Bill sensed that a door had opened for him. The challenge was to use his fame to fatten his empty purse.

Chapter 6

On Stage and Off

Bill made his first visit to New York in the spring of 1872. Ned Buntline took him to see a play based on his exploits. *Buffalo Bill, King of the Border Men* was one long tall tale. Bill drew the loudest cheers when he walked on stage to take a bow.

Buntline argued that Bill should become an actor. He promised to write a play tailored to his talents. Bill left to rejoin the Fifth Cavalry without giving him an answer.

As Buntline could see, Bill Cody was a performer. In his role as Buffalo Bill, he stood for the ideal Western man. He could ride and shoot, scout and hunt. His word was his bond. If he had a dollar, he would share it. He liked whiskey but never seemed to get drunk.

Working as a scout and guide kept Bill away from home for many months at a time. His wife, Louisa, still yearned for a more peaceful existence. Also, she was jealous of the women who threw themselves at him. Yet it was Louisa who sewed his colorful costumes. She also raised their three children. When Bill was home, he spoiled Arta, Kit, and Orra Maude.

Bill met Buntline in Chicago that winter. *Scouts of the Prairie* opened a few days later to a packed house. When the curtain went up on December 16, Bill forgot his lines. Buntline saved the day by asking, "Where have you been, Bill?" Bill told a few stories and warmed to the task. Before long, the stage was filled with gunsmoke. Actors dressed as American Indians died by the dozen. The critics thought the play was dreadful. The audience loved it.

The play ran until June 1873. In September, Bill opened a new play, *Scouts of the Plains*. Bill Hickok, now a famous lawman, took Buntline's place. When bored, Wild Bill fired blanks at the legs of his fellow actors. The powder burns set them to hopping wildly. Wild Bill left the stage after that single season.

Bill bought a home in Rochester, New York. He spent the summer of 1875 there with his family. Tragedy struck the following April while Bill was on tour. He rushed home when five-year-old Kit fell ill with scarlet fever. The boy died in his arms a few hours later.

Buffalo Bill (center) poses for a photo with Ned Buntline (left) and John Omohundro. Buntline convinced Bill that he should try stage acting. Bill appeared in his first performance of *Scouts of the Prairie* on December 16, 1872.

In June 1876, trouble was brewing in the Dakota Territory. On June 17, the Sioux fought off General George Crook. Eight days later, General George Custer met Sitting Bull at the Little Bighorn River. In a crushing defeat, Custer's troops died to the last man. Bill was called west to scout for the Fifth Cavalry.

A thousand Cheyenne were riding to join Sitting Bull. The Fifth moved to head them off near War Bonnet Creek. On July 17, Bill led a small force in a flanking attack. He and a subchief named Yellow Hair opened fire at the same moment. Bill's shot smashed the Cheyenne's leg and killed his pony. Yellow Hair's slug missed. Bill's horse stumbled and fell, but he rolled clear. Yellow Hair aimed, fired—and missed again. Bill's return shot found its mark.

Bill saw that Yellow Hair had tied a blonde scalp to his war bonnet. In his fury, Bill scalped the fallen subchief. Holding the war bonnet over his head, he cried, "The first scalp for Custer!" That brief firefight ended the campaign. The outgunned Cheyenne went back to their homes.

Bill appeared in a new play that fall. He called it *The Red Right Hand*, or *Bill's First Scalp for Custer.* On stage, the shoot-out with Yellow Hair turned into a hand-to-hand duel. The next year's play was *Boy Chief of the Plains*. The public did not care that each play was much like the one before. Bill made enough money to buy a ranch near North Platte, Nebraska.

Bill knew his plays were rather silly. He dreamed of showing people the true West. His chance came in 1882. North Platte put him in charge of its Fourth of July show. Bill's Old Glory Blow-Out featured bronco riding, a stagecoach holdup, and a buffalo hunt. The applause convinced him that this was his type of show.

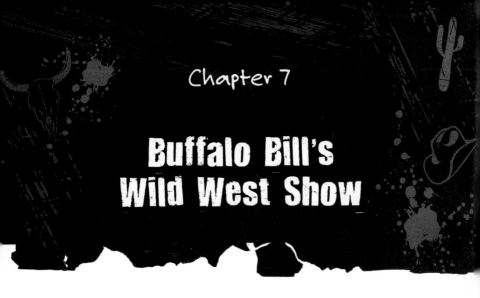

Chapter 7

Buffalo Bill's Wild West Show

B ill put all his talent and cash into building a Wild West show. He and his partner, Dr. W. F. Carver, planned to "take the prairies and the Injuns and everything else right to 'em." They hired cowboys, American Indians, and sharpshooters. Their agents rounded up a buffalo herd and bought bucking broncos. The livestock and equipment filled six boxcars.

The show opened in Omaha in May 1883. Posters bragged, "The Green Sward Our Carpet, Azure Canopy Our Canvas, No Tinsel, No Gilding, No Humbug!" On show day, a cowboy band led a dramatic parade through the streets. The public, avid readers of dime novels, raced to buy tickets. Buffalo Bill was bringing them the real West!

The opening did not go smoothly. Some of the riders had spent too much time in the town's saloons.

Even so, the crowd loved the show's wild energy. The cowboys showed off their riding and roping skills. American Indians raced bareback. The stagecoach robbery brought down the house. Bill thrilled his fans with a new act. Firing while riding at a gallop, he shattered glass balls thrown high by a second rider. In his first appearance, he hit eighty-seven out of one hundred balls.

A stressed-out Carver left after the first season. Showman Nate Salsbury moved in as Bill's new partner. With Salsbury taking care of the business end, Bill was free to improve the show. He bought new equipment and hired new acts. One key addition was Johnny Baker. Back in Omaha, the nine-year-old had attached himself to Bill. In turn, Bill treated Johnny like a son. Later, billed as the Cowboy Kid, Johnny put on a sharpshooting act.

Wild West fans could always count on five spectacles. Each year, painted American Indians performed war dances. Settlers defended their log cabin. Buffalo Bill saved the Deadwood stage. Pony Express riders carried the mail. A grand buffalo hunt always brought the crowd to its feet. Special effects included prairie fires, stampedes, and a cyclone.

Bill dressed to fit the popular image of a western scout. He wore his wide-brimmed white hat at a jaunty angle. A scarlet shirt set off his fringed white buckskin jacket. A matching sash circled his waist. Thigh-high black boots gleamed over white trousers. At his side, he carried his trusty rifle. He took equal care in making the show look real. Author Mark Twain was convinced. Twain wrote: "Down to its smallest details the Show is genuine."

Annie Oakley joined Buffalo Bill's Wild West Show in 1885. Many considered her the best sharpshooter in the world. She became a main attraction in Bill's show.

In 1885, Buffalo Bill's Wild West Show added two stars. The first was sharpshooter Annie Oakley. Born in Ohio in 1860, Annie began shooting at age eight. At fifteen, she outshot marksman Frank Butler. Butler soon became her husband and manager. Bill told his cast, "This little Missie here . . . she's the only white woman with our show. I want you boys to welcome and protect her."

Annie was an artist with a rifle. At thirty paces, she could slice a playing card held edgewise. Women covered their eyes when Frank held up a dime between two fingers—but Annie never missed. She even went Bill one better. She smashed flying glass balls, too— while sighting over her shoulder with a mirror.

Sitting Bull, the victor of Little Bighorn, also appeared that season. At first, the aging chief had refused to join the show. Then Bill's agent spotted a photo of Annie in the chief's tepee. Sitting Bull, who called Annie "Little Sure Shot," had seen her perform. Told he would see her every day, Sitting Bull signed on for $50 a week. He also made good money selling autographed photos. When crowds booed him for his part in Custer's defeat, he ignored them. At season's end, Bill gave Sitting Bull a gray trick horse and a white sombrero.

This photo of Sitting Bull and Buffalo Bill was taken in 1885. Sitting Bull earned $50 per week working for Buffalo Bill's show.

In 1884, the show had nearly collapsed after a riverboat sank. Much of the equipment ended up on the bottom of the Mississippi. Rebuilding was slow work. The 1885 season, however, turned a $100,000 profit. As he neared forty, Bill looked for new worlds to conquer.

Chapter 8

Performing for the Queen

In 1887, the people of Europe were reading and talking about the Wild West. Sure of a warm welcome, Buffalo Bill took his show to Great Britain. If the British wanted western romance, he would give it to them.

Traveling to Europe meant a seventeen-day ocean voyage. The animals may have had the best of the trip. Most of the two-legged performers were seasick. Certain they were dying, the American Indians chanted their death songs. Annie Oakley proved to be one of the better sailors. For several days, she had the ship's dining room almost to herself.

When the ship docked, the British waived some of their laws. The show's horses, buffalo, wild steers, elk, and mules were quarantined briefly. The cast members were allowed to keep their firearms. Officials did draw the line at live bullets. Ammunition was stored at an army post and was issued as needed.

The show set up camp at Earl's Court on the west side of London. Rehearsals began in a huge twenty-thousand-seat arena. April rains chilled cast and crew. At night, they huddled around coal fires in large, wooden-floored tents. To build interest, Bill gave away free tickets. The passes, which were prepunched, became known as "Annie Oakleys." They looked as though Annie had used them as targets.

Edward, Prince of Wales, previewed the show. The future king was entranced. His praise led his mother, Queen Victoria, to ask Bill to perform at Windsor Castle. Bill had to turn her down. The show was too big to move for just one performance. Victoria then surprised everyone. She announced that she would come to Earl's Court. This would be her first theater outing in twenty-six years. She had been in seclusion since the death of her husband.

Queen Victoria's coach rolled into Earl's Court on May 11. The queen, a stout who was then sixty-seven years old, took her seat in a box trimmed with flags. Bill opened the show by carrying the Stars and Stripes into the arena. The queen stood and bowed. With that bow, she became the first British ruler ever to salute

BUFFALO BILL'S WILD WEST
AND CONGRESS OF ROUGH RIDERS OF THE WORLD.

ARAB HORSEMEN

COL. W. F. CODY
"BUFFALO BILL"
WILL APPEAR
AT EVERY PERFORMANCE

THE REAL SONS OF THE SOUDAN, WHOSE BRAWN & MUSCLE HAVE AMAZED THE WORLD, VIVIDLY ILLUSTRATING THEIR FEATS OF STRENGTH, MARVELOUS HORSEMANSHIP, ATHLETIC ACHIEVEMENTS, GUN SPINNING AND PYRAMID BUILDING

Buffalo Bill took his show across the Atlantic to Europe and performed for Queen Victoria. This poster promotes Buffalo Bill's Wild West Show during his tour of Europe in 1899.

the American flag. Queen Victoria had planned to stay only an hour. Caught up in the drama, she stayed for the entire seventy-five minutes. Afterward, she chatted with Bill, Annie, and Chief Red Shirt.

In June, Victoria asked to see the show again. Bill took his best acts to Windsor Castle for the command performance. The highlight came when he picked up the reins of the Deadwood stagecoach. Riding inside were the kings of Denmark, Greece, Belgium, and Saxony. The Prince of Wales sat beside him on the driver's seat. As the stagecoach jolted forward, a band of American Indians swooped past. Riding bareback, they yelled and fired blanks. The ride gave birth to a popular joke. The stage, Bill liked to say, had carried Four Kings and the Royal Joker.

The cowboys made their rodeo tricks look easy. England's top riders said they could stick on the broncs, too. The best lasted only thirty seconds before being bucked off. Two of the cowboys entered a six-day race against two English cyclists. For eight hours each day, the four riders circled a track at Islington. The cowboys used thirty horses, changing mounts each hour. When the race ended, the cowboys were two laps ahead.

The show moved north in the fall. At Salford, Bill and Nate Salsbury opened "the largest theater ever seen." The ten-thousand-seat indoor arena was heated by steam and lighted by electricity. The cast performed in front of a huge painted backdrop of the western plains. The local paper reported: "Buffalo Bill has come, we have seen, and he has conquered."

The homesick cast sailed for the United States in May 1888. The voyage was marred only by the death of Bill's horse, Old Charlie. The show reopened a few weeks later on Staten Island, New York. Not to be outdone by a British queen, President Grover Cleveland attended the opening.

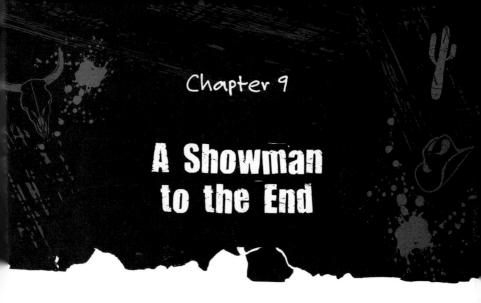

Chapter 9

A Showman to the End

In the fall of 1888, Bill rested at his ranch near North Platte. His life with Louisa had reached a low point. Their disputes centered on the fact that Bill would not, could not, settle down. Louisa, in turn, disliked travel. In time, they no longer spoke.

In 1889, a Wild West fever swept Europe. Bill took his show to France, Spain, and Italy. Pope Leo XIII blessed the members of the cast. After a sellout year in Germany, the show played Holland and Belgium. Stories spread that the American Indians were badly treated. The rumors were false. Like the rest of the cast, they simply wanted to go home.

Bill took the show home, but he was not finished in Europe. By May 1892, he was back in London, staging a third performance for Queen Victoria. Russian Cossacks and Argentine gauchos now rode beside

American cowboys. Bill called the new show the Congress of the Rough Riders of the World.

The great showman had other interests as well. One was a new ranch in the Bighorn basin of Wyoming. In 1895, he helped lay out the nearby town that would bear his name. Six years later, the first train chugged into Cody. Bill joined in the celebration. When war broke out with Spain in 1898, fifty-two-year-old Bill Cody tried to join up. The fighting ended before the army took him up on his offer.

In 1903, Bill bought into a mine near Oracle, Arizona. Engineers promised a rich strike of gold, tungsten, and lead. For seven months, miners drilled around the clock. When at last they hit a vein of ore, it proved to be low grade. By 1912, $500,000 of Bill's cash had vanished down the Campo Bonito mine.

At age sixty-six, Buffalo Bill was wearing out. His health was poor. His debts were mounting. He talked of retiring, but he could not afford to quit.

An old friend, Major Gordon Lillie, talked him into making a three-year "farewell tour." The first year of the tour went well, then gate receipts fell. The public was learning to prefer movie versions of the Wild West. Bill's act no longer drew the crowds.

As the years sped past, Bill found himself in financial trouble. To pay off his debts, he had to keep working even as his health worsened.

Early in 1913, Bill borrowed $20,000. When he could not repay the loan, he had to auction off his animals and wagons.

Next, he tried his hand at making a movie. For one big scene, he hired American Indians to restage the Battle of Wounded Knee. Just before the cameras started rolling, Bill heard a chilling rumor. The young warriors wanted to avenge the 1890 massacre. Instead of firing blanks, they were planning to use real bullets.

Bill talked to the older chiefs, who kept the hotheads under control. In February 1914, Bill showed "The Indian Wars" to members of Congress. Then he took the film on the road for a brief tour.

To pay off old debts, Bill traveled with the Sells-Floto Circus. On his bad days, he had to be helped onto his horse. On the saddle, he straightened his back. Only then did he ride into the spotlight. He made his final appearance in November 1916.

Too ill to travel, Bill spent his last days in Denver. Death came on January 10, 1917. His friends knew he wanted to be buried on Cedar Mountain above Cody. Louisa, however, claimed that he had changed his mind. She buried him on Denver's Lookout Mountain. To honor their founder, the people of Cody built their own memorial. Their twelve-foot bronze statue shows Bill astride his black horse, Smokey.

Like all great heroes, Bill is still with us. He speaks across the years of courage, loyalty, and independence. Mounted on Buckskin Joe, he charges toward us. He holds a rifle in one hand, the reins in the other. His long hair streams behind him. It is an image that will last as long as memories of the Wild West endure.

Glossary

abolitionist—Someone who opposed the practice of slavery.

bankrupt—Financially ruined. A business goes bankrupt when it has more debts than assets.

broncos—Horses that have not been broken for riding.

buckskin—The skin of a male deer. Western scouts favored clothing made of buckskin.

cavalry—In Buffalo Bill's day, army units mounted on horseback. Today's cavalry soldiers ride in tanks and armored cars.

Civil War—The war between the Union, the northern states, and the Confederacy, the southern states, 1861–1865.

command performance—A show staged at the request of a king, queen, or other high-ranking figure.

constable—A law officer charged with keeping the peace in a town or village.

consumption—A common name for tuberculosis in the 1800s.

corral—A fenced area used to keep horses and cattle from straying.

czar—The emperor of imperial Russia.

dime novels—Low-cost magazines that printed popular fiction during the late 1800s.

dude—A western term used to describe a city-bred visitor.

flank attack—An attack on the left or right side of an enemy's formation.

greenbacks—A slang term for United States paper money.

lasso—A long rope with a running noose at one end. Cowboys use lassos to catch horses and cattle.

mochila—The leather sheet used by Pony Express riders as a saddle cover and mail pouch.

Pony Express—An overland mail service that relied on relays of riders and horses to carry the mail.

quarantine—Enforced isolation of animals or people suspected of carrying a contagious disease.

roan—A bay, chestnut, or sorrel horse whose coat is sprinkled with white or gray.

saddletree—The wooden frame that gives a saddle its shape and stability.

scout—A skilled tracker and guide. Scouts ride ahead of a larger force to gather information about the terrain and the dangers that lie ahead.

seclusion—Staying hidden from public view.

sharpshooter—A marksman who demonstrates a high level of skill with a pistol or rifle.

sombrero—A Spanish name for a wide-brimmed hat that was popular in the Old West.

Further Reading

Books

Goodman, Michael E. *Buffalo Bill Cody.* Mankato, Minn.: Creative Education, 2006.

Haugen, Brenda. *Annie Oakley: American Sharpshooter.* Minneapolis, Minn.: Compass Point Books, 2007.

Reis, Ronald A. *Buffalo Bill Cody.* New York: Chelsea House Publishers, 2010.

Silate, Jennifer. *Little Sure Shot: Annie Oakley and Buffalo Bill's Wild West Show.* New York: Rosen Publishing Group, 2004.

Stefoff, Rebecca. *The Wild West.* New York: Marshall Cavendish Benchmark, 2007.

Internet Addresses

Buffalo Bill Historical Center
<http://www.bbhc.org/>

The Buffalo Bill Museum and Grave
<http://www.buffalobill.org/>

PBS—New Perspectives on the West: William F. Cody
<http://www.pbs.org/weta/thewest/people/a_c/buffalobill.htm>

Index